Read & Respond

Ages
7–11

SECTION 1

Diary of a Wimpy Kid

Teachers' notes 3

SECTION 2

Guided reading

Teachers' notes 4

SECTION 3

Shared reading

Teachers' notes 7
Photocopiable extracts 8

SECTION 4

Plot, character and setting

Activity notes 11
Photocopiable activities 15

SECTION 5

Talk about it

Activity notes 19
Photocopiable activities 22

SECTION 6

Get writing

Activity notes 25
Photocopiable activities 28

SECTION 7

Assessment

Teachers' notes and activity 31
Photocopiable activity 32

D1477891

PAGE
1

Read & Respond

Ages
7~11

Author: Pam Dowson

Commissioning Editor: Rachel Mackinnon

Development Editor: Marion Archer

Assistant Editor: Rachel Coombs

Series Designer: Anna Oliwa

Designer: Anna Oliwa

Text © 2012, Pam Dowson © 2012, Scholastic Ltd

Designed using Adobe InDesign

Published by Scholastic Ltd,
Book End, Range Road, Witney,
Oxfordshire OX29 0YD
www.scholastic.co.uk

Printed by Bell & Bain
2 3 4 5 6 7 8 9   4 5 6 7 8 9 0 1

British Library Cataloguing-in-Publication Data
A catalogue record for this book is available from
the British Library.

ISBN 978-1407-12727-9

Acknowledgements

The publishers gratefully acknowledge permission to reproduce the following copyright material: **Penguin Books** for the use of the cover, text extracts and illustrations from *Diary of a Wimpy Kid* by Jeff Kinney. Text and illustrations © 2007, Jeff Kinney (2007, Harry N Abrams).
Every effort has been made to trace copyright holders for the works reproduced in this book, and the publishers apologise for any inadvertent omissions.

Diary of a Wimpy Kid

About the book

Diary of a Wimpy Kid is a novel written in the form of series of diary entries by the character Greg Heffley. Greg is an ordinary American child, full of bright ideas which somehow always manage to backfire; for Greg nothing ever seems to go according to plan. He records one school year's worth of the key events of his life in his journal (he's most insistent that it is a journal, not a diary). As Greg explains, his motivation for writing a journal is that it will be an invaluable, time-saving resource when he achieves his aim of becoming rich and famous. Through his journal pages, presented as handwriting on lined paper for authenticity, we get to know Greg's family – Mom, Dad, older brother Rodrick (with his love of heavy-metal music), and annoying younger brother Manny – along with Rowley, his best friend (for most of the book, at least) who is more law-abiding and quietly more successful than Greg.

The journal runs from September through to the following June, during which time the reader shares Greg's various escapades including: his ill-fated involvement with the school play, his attempts at wrestling, snowman-building, comic-strip creation and his plan for successful inclusion in the school yearbook. Sadly and inevitably, all his efforts are doomed to failure, but Greg is not easily discouraged. Despite regular setbacks, his resilience, self-belief and general optimism carry him on to his next 'great' idea.

Themes explored in this novel include the trials and tribulations of friendships, family relationships, truth and lies, coping with failure and dealing with the need to be popular and successful among one's peers. There are also clear links with journal writing and comic strip creation.

About the author

Jeff Kinney was born in 1971 in Fort Washington, Maryland, USA. At university he created a comic strip for the college newspaper, called *Igdoof*. After his studies he became an online game developer and designer.

Kinney tells us, on his website (www.wimpykid.com) that his goal was *to write a book that made people laugh*. He thinks *Greg is self-centred and can be kind of clueless. I don't think Greg is a bad kid, necessarily; but like all of us, he has his faults. Hopefully readers will understand that Greg's imperfections are what make him funny.*

Kinney spent four years generating ideas for the story of *Diary of a Wimpy Kid* and another four years writing and illustrating. It took a further year to get the book into print but once published, it quickly became a *New York Times* bestseller.

In 2009, Jeff Kinney was named as one of *Time* magazine's Most Influential People in the World. He lives in Massachusetts, USA, with his wife and two sons.

Facts and figures

Originally published online on the *Funbrain* children's website, where Kinney worked.
More than 1300 daily entries appeared over a nine-month period, generating over 80 million visits.
The print version was first published in 2007.
By 2010 there were more than 42 million copies of the series in print worldwide.
It was adapted into a film in 2010, combining animation and live-action.

Guided reading

Introduction

With the children, examine the front cover and talk about the subtitle *A novel in cartoons*, ensuring the children understand the word 'novel'. Ask: *What do you think 'Wimpy' means?* Link this to the cartoon boy. Explain that the story is set in America, where Middle School is usually for children aged between 11 and 14. Open the first few pages of the book, drawing attention to the lined paper and handwriting-style font. Ask: *Why do you think the book is presented in this way?* (To provide authenticity.)

September

Read the first four journal entries with the children. This first section introduces Greg and explains why he starts to keep a journal. Note the use of the first person, and ask for examples of informal language (such as *jerk, gonna, dumbest, I guess, us guys*). Discuss the use of cartoons. Ask: *How do you think the cartoons help to tell the story?* (They give more information, are easy to interpret, and make the book more fun.) It is the beginning of the school year and Greg talks about what is important for him at Middle School, which includes finding the right seat, being popular and being in the right groups. Ask: *What do you think are the important things to get right at the start of the school year?*

Move on to read the next five entries. Here we start to become acquainted with other key characters (Mom, Dad, Manny, Rowley, Fregley and Rodrick). Invite the children to explain how Greg feels about each of these people, finding evidence in the text to support suggestions. For example, Rowley can annoy Greg because he still behaves as he did in elementary school, but Greg also likes having him around so he can play the tricks on Rowley that Rodrick plays on *him*. As a group, make bulleted lists of the characteristics of each key person.

Now read the remaining entries for September. Ask: *Can you see two different ways that block capitals are used in this section?* (In the main text capitals are used for emphasis, such as in *TOTALLY*. Capitals are also in the cartoon captions which is the accepted font style for comic strips.) Talk about the different ways that Mom and Dad deal with Greg's misdemeanours. (Mom thinks about punishments for longer, while Dad deals with it, then it's forgotten.) Ask: *Whose way would you prefer, and why?* Compare Dad's and Greg's posters for student government. Ask: *Which would most likely attract votes and why? What would Dad think of Greg's posters, and what might he do about it?*

October

With the children, read the first three entries for October. Look at the phrase *Those guys were charging five bucks a pop*. If they don't understand the language, explain that this means the boys were charging five American dollars to go in the haunted house. This episode provides an example of how Greg's good ideas always go wrong. Examine the plan and poster, and talk about how the boys might have realised it wouldn't work. (They were too ambitious, there wasn't enough time and it is not possible to have live sharks.)

Continue reading up to the end of October. With the children, make a list of all the things that go wrong for Greg when he goes trick-or-treating. (They include: Rowley's costume, taking Manny, the high-school kids attacking them, Dad spraying them with water.) Ask: *Have you ever had plans that went wrong?* Focus on the attack by the high-school kids. Ask: *Do you think Greg and Rowley should tell their parents about this? What would you do?*

November

Read the first five entries for November. There are a number of words and phrases in this section that the children may be unfamiliar with because of the use of American English, and language specific to wrestling and weight training. Read the phrase *I would have traded for Benny Wells in a heartbeat*. Check the children know what *traded* means (swapped), and what *in a heartbeat* suggests (very quickly). Ask: *What might Greg eat if he was* loading up on junk food? Can the children work out what is meant by the phrase *shirts and skins*? Encourage them to use the cartoons to help them. (One team wears shirts, the other wear no shirts.)

Work through this section together, listing any words or phrases that the children find puzzling, and talk about what they might mean, using the context to help. Words the children might suggest are: *Phys Ed* (PE), *pile drivers* (a wrestling move), *ripped* (a fine physique), *barbell* (sports' equipment) and *reps* (repetitions). The children could make a glossary of unusual words, adding to it as they continue reading the book.

Next, read the short entry about the geography quiz, which seems at first to be an isolated event, but it sets the seeds for Greg's desire to get his own back on Patty Farrell, who ruins his chances of doing well in the test. Read to the end of November where Greg reluctantly tries out for a part in the school play. Do the children empathise with him? Ask: *How does Greg plan to mess things up in the play for Patty Farrell?* (He wants to throw apples at her in his tree costume.)

December

With the children, read the first three entries for December. Several things happen to embarrass Greg when he takes part in the school play. Can the children identify what these are? (Having to sing, Rodrick watching with a video camera, Manny calling out his nickname *Bubby*.) At the end of the section, Greg says he was *entertained* by the play, but his family were not, as their cartoon faces show us. Ask the children why this was. (The play was ruined as Greg and the other trees threw apples, breaking Patty Farrell's glasses.)

Continue reading to the end of December. Through no fault of his own, Greg does not have a good Christmas. Ask: *How do you feel about Greg having such a disappointing Christmas?* (They may feel sorry for him.) Encourage them to cite evidence from the text to support their opinions. (He does not get any of the presents he hoped for, while his brother gets everything and his most hoped-for present is mistakenly given to someone

else.) In contrast, after Christmas, Greg is up to his old tricks, terrorising his little brother with a pretend spider. What do the children think of this? Do they agree with his punishment?

January

Read through all of the entries for January. This section begins with Greg devising a game which results in Rowley breaking his hand. Ask the children what their feelings are towards Greg after this. Greg seems very selfish as, rather than being sorry for causing the injury, he actually appears jealous of the attention Rowley receives with his arm in plaster. At the end of this month, Greg signs up for Safety Patrol. Can the children explain what this role involves? (This is a responsible position in which people help others.) Ask them to examine Greg's reasoning. (He only applies to benefit himself, he wants hot chocolate privileges and to miss Pre-Algebra lessons.)

February

Continue reading to the end of February. The main event in this month is the cartoonist competition. At first, Greg and Rowley work together to create a cartoon, but they fall out. Greg enters his own comic strip and, to make sure he wins, he hides a lot of the other children's entries. What do the children make of these actions? (Dishonest and cheating.) When Greg wins the competition, the teacher changes parts of the cartoon. Ask: *Why do you think the teacher changes Greg's comic?* (He probably found it offensive and he wants to get his own messages across.) *How does Greg feel?*

March

After reading the events in Greg's March entries, invite the children to closely examine Greg's behaviour. We discover in this section that Greg abused his Safety Patrol role by scaring the kindergartners with worms. Then, when Rowley is mistakenly blamed for this incident, Greg refuses to own up and clear his friend. Greg

Guided reading

doesn't think how his actions might affect others, or accept responsibility afterwards when things go wrong. Do the children agree that Greg is self-centred and has an apparent disregard for others? Do they understand Rowley's reaction? Would they have gone to the teacher?

April

Continue reading through the entries for April. The worm incident has resulted in the boys falling out. After losing Rowley's friendship, we see how having a best friend and being popular with his classmates are important to Greg as he seeks to reinstate himself. Ask: *What do you think of Greg as a friend? Would you have him as a friend? Why?* Greg says that he needs to talk to Rowley about loyalty, but he shows himself to be disloyal. Throughout the diary Greg hasn't mentioned any other friends, so his only choice is the unpopular Fregley. Ask: *Why do you think Greg doesn't seem to have other friends?* Without a best friend, Greg turns his attention to increasing his popularity with others by striving unsuccessfully to become elected Class Clown in the yearbook. Ask: *Why does he want this title? How does he plan to win it? Is Greg trying to hide his loneliness?*

May

After reading the May entries, invite the children to explain how Greg feels when his Mom is the substitute teacher. (Embarrassed and upset because he can't play his prank.) Do the children understand how Greg's disappointment increases when he discovers Rowley is the new cartoonist?

Focus on the incident with the teenagers. Ask for suggestions about the missing word and why Greg is reluctant to write that Rowley had to EAT the cheese (he doesn't want anyone to ever know). Explain that Greg's behaviour at this point demonstrates that he can be a loyal friend, when he takes the blame for moving the cheese, thereby 'catching' the *Cheese Touch*. Discuss how the author planted the idea at the start, so he could surprise us at the end, giving us a chance to see another side of Greg.

June

Read the remaining month's entries and encourage the children to explain how and why Rowley has forgiven Greg. Ask: *How does Greg feel about having the* Cheese Touch*?* (He seems to look on the bright side. Is he just happy to have Rowley back?) At the end of the story, Rowley is elected as Class Clown, a role that Greg had hoped for. Ask: *How do you think Greg feels about Rowley being Class Clown? Do you think they will still be friends after this?* (Greg might be annoyed for a while but he clearly missed Rowley so is unlikely to want to lose his friendship again.)

Shared reading

Extract 1

● Display Extract 1 and ask the children what they notice about the layout. Draw attention to the very short, sometimes one sentence, paragraphs. Explain that this reflects the informal, chatty style of the writing, as though Greg was speaking directly to us.

● Highlight the words *EXACTLY* and *BEGGED*. Ask why these two words are in block capitals, and model reading them with emphasis.

● Discuss how the cartoon reinforces and further emphasises Greg's begging. (It shows Greg pleading on his knees.)

● Highlight *"well-rounded"* and read the sentence in which it occurs. Do the class understand what the word means here? Discuss how the phrase *trying different things* gives a clue to its meaning.

● Invite the children to pick out parts of the text that tell us about Mom and Dad, compare these characters and make a class list. (For instance, keen to support their son, want him to be involved in school events, eager for him to gain experiences, Mom wins the argument).

Extract 2

● Read aloud the opening sentence of Extract 2. Talk about how this direct approach involves the reader immediately. It also gives us several pieces of information in one sentence (highlight *in my room, 9:00 p.m.*, and *New Year's Eve*) as well as the implication that Greg must have done something wrong.

● Highlight the words *horsing around* in the second paragraph. Can the children suggest any synonyms? (For instance, messing about, playing or fooling around.)

● Next, focus on the third and fourth paragraphs and invite the children to discuss what they, and the cartoon, tell us about Greg's personality and power over Manny. Ask: *How would you describe the siblings' relationship?* (Turbulent and difficult. Greg calls Manny a *fool*.)

● Read to the end. Ask them to suggest sections that show us Greg does not have as much power over Manny as he thinks. (For example, *I knew I was in big trouble, Manny told Mom I made him, I got sent to bed at 7:00*.)

Extract 3

● Cover the lower half of Extract 3, from and including the cartoon. Then read aloud the displayed text. Highlight *"disrespected the badge"* and explain that this means Greg had done something wrong when in a position of honour and authority.

● Underline the sentence *So I decided to have some fun with the kids* and ask the class for suggestions. Then reveal the cartoon. Is this what the children expected? Is it right to call this *fun*? (It seems mean/cruel.)

● Reveal and read the rest of the extract. Highlight the sentences beginning with *And*. Explain that we don't usually start sentences with 'and', but it works here, mainly because of the writing style which is more like the spoken word.

● Invite the children to discuss what this incident tells us about Greg. What would the teachers think? How would Rowley feel when he discovers that he had been blamed for something Greg had actually done? Why doesn't Greg confess? (He is quite selfish, caring about his hot chocolate privileges rather than clearing Rowley.)

Extract 1

NOVEMBER: Thursday

Tonight Mom came up to my room, and she had a flyer in her hand. As soon as I saw it, I knew EXACTLY what it was.

It was an announcement that the school is having tryouts for a winter play. Man, I should have thrown that thing out when I saw it on the kitchen table.

I BEGGED her not to make me sign up. Those school plays are always musicals, and the last thing I need is to have to sing a solo in front of the whole school.

But all my begging seemed to do was make Mom more sure I should do it.

Mom said the only way I was going to be "well-rounded" was by trying different things.

Dad came in my room to see what was going on. I told Dad that Mom was making me sign up for the school play, and that if I had to start going to play practices, it would totally mess up my weight-lifting schedule.

I knew that would make Dad take my side. Dad and Mom argued for a few minutes, but Dad was no match for Mom.

So that means tomorrow I've got to audition for the school play.

Text and illustrations © 2007, Jeff Kinney.

SCHOLASTIC
www.scholastic.co.uk

Extract 2

DECEMBER: *New Year's Eve*

In case you're wondering what I'm doing in my room at 9:00 p.m. on New Year's Eve, let me fill you in.

Earlier today, me and Manny were horsing around in the basement. I found a tiny black ball of thread on the carpet, and I told Manny it was a spider.

Then I held it over him pretending that I was going to make him eat it.

Right when I was about to let Manny go, he slapped my hand and made me drop the thread. And guess what? That fool swallowed it.

Well, Manny completely lost his mind. He ran upstairs to where Mom as, and I knew I was in big trouble.

Manny told Mom I made him eat a spider. I told her there was no spider, and that it was just a tiny ball of thread.

Mom brought Manny over to the kitchen table. Then she put a seed, a raisin and a grape on a plate and told Manny to point to the thing that was the closest in size to the piece of thread he swallowed.

Manny took a while to look over the things on the plate.

Then he walked over to the refrigerator and pulled out an orange.

So that's why I got sent to bed at 7:00 and I'm not downstairs watching the New Year's Eve special on TV.

And that's also why my only New Year's resolution is to never play with Manny again.

Extract 3

MARCH: *Wednesday*

Apparently Mr Winsky got a call from a parent who said they witnessed Rowley "terrorizing" the kindergartners when he was supposed to be walking them home from school. And Mr Winsky was really mad about it.

Rowley said Mr Winsky yelled at him for about ten minutes and said his actions "disrespected the badge".

You know, I think I might just know what this is all about. Last week, Rowley had to take a quiz during fourth period, so I walked the kindergartners home on my own.

It had rained that morning, and there were a lot of worms on the pavement. So I decided to have some fun with the kids.

But some neighbourhood lady saw what I was doing, and she yelled at me from her front porch.

It was Mrs Irvine, who is friends with Rowley's mom. She must have thought I was Rowley, because I was borrowing his hat. And I wasn't about to correct her, either.

I forgot about the whole incident until today.

Anyway, Mr Winsky told Rowley he's going to have to apologize to the kindergartners tomorrow morning, and that he's suspended from Patrols for a week.

I knew I should probably just tell Mr Winsky it was me who chased the kids with the worms. But I wasn't ready to set the record straight just yet. I knew if I confessed, I'd lose my hot chocolate privileges. And that right there was enough to make me keep quiet for the time being.

Text and illustrations © 2007, Jeff Kinney.

Plot, character and setting

The Cheese Touch

> **Objective:** To interrogate texts to deepen and clarify understanding and response.
> **What you need:** Copies of *Diary of a Wimpy Kid*, writing materials and internet access.
> **Cross-curricular links:** PSHE, ICT.

What to do

● With the children, discuss common superstitions, such as walking under ladders, counting magpies and avoiding cracks in the pavement. Talk about how superstitions can affect people.
● Read the first Wednesday entry in September – about the school superstition surrounding a piece of discarded cheese. Explain that the *Cooties* is slang for when someone is said to be 'infected' with a contagious unknown disease.

Can the children find any evidence for the *Cheese Touch* being real? (There is none – it's pure superstition.)
● Arrange the children into small groups and challenge them to use books and the internet to research commonly-held superstitions.
● Bring the class together to listen to the children's findings.

> **Differentiation**
> **For older/more confident learners:** Encourage the children to create a PowerPoint presentation of their findings about common superstitions.
> **For younger/less confident learners:** Allow the children to focus on researching one or two common superstitions and provide them with a list of useful websites to visit.

How to be popular

> **Objective:** To infer characters' feelings in fiction and consequences in logical explanations.
> **What you need:** Copies of *Diary of a Wimpy Kid* and photocopiable page 15.
> **Cross-curricular link:** PSHE.

What to do

● Read the first entry for September to the class. Ask: *What does this tell us about how Greg is feeling?* (He wants to be popular and doesn't want to look a fool in front of older children.) Rowley seems less concerned about being popular. Ask why this might be. (He may be unaware of the competition, unlike Greg, or is just not bothered.)
● Write the headings 'What you do' and 'What you own' on the board. Ask: *What makes people popular?* Encourage suggestions, including those from the novel to put under each heading (such as fast runner, good at sports, trendy clothes, lots of

money, and so on). Discuss whether any of these are a good basis for being popular. Do any make you a good person, worthy of popularity? Would being a poor runner, or not having expensive clothes make someone unpopular?
● Greg tells us that he is trying to be careful about his image at middle school. Hand out photocopiable page 15 and invite the children to complete it, deciding what actions can improve Greg's popularity. There will probably be a variety of responses, which can be used as the basis for a class discussion.

> **Differentiation**
> **For older/more confident learners:** Encourage the children to add ideas of their own to both lists, and give reasons for their choices.
> **For younger/less confident learners:** Allow the children to work in pairs and concentrate on categorising half of the list.

Plot, character and setting

How embarrassing!

> **Objective:** To empathise with characters and debate moral dilemmas portrayed in texts.
> **What you need:** A copy of Extract 1 (from page 8).
> **Cross-curricular links:** PSHE, drama.

What to do

● Start a discussion about things which the children find embarrassing, such as parents drawing attention to them in public or being unable to answer a question in class. How would they describe how this makes them feel? Is there ever anything they can do about it?

● Display and read Extract 1. Discuss Greg's anticipation of feeling embarrassed. Ask: *Why might he dread being in the school play?* (Maybe he has sung in front of the whole school before or he believes other children will laugh at him.)

● Draw attention to the strength of the word *BEGGED* and the accompanying cartoon. (They show just how desperate Greg is.)

● Greg seems to have no control over what happens to him; his parents are making the decisions, even though he tries to influence his dad to take his side. With the class, make two lists, one for the things children can decide for themselves, and one for those which their parents decide.

> **Differentiation**
> **For older/more confident learners:** In pairs, invite the children to devise and enact a role play where a child is embarrassed by a parent.
> **For younger/less confident learners:** In small groups, ask the children to discuss and list things that might embarrass someone, both in and out of school.

Actions speak louder than words

> **Objective:** To identify features that writers use to provoke readers' reactions.
> **What you need:** A copy of Extract 2 (from page 9) and writing materials.
> **Cross-curricular links:** PSHE, maths, drama.

What to do

● Display Extract 2 and draw attention to the first-person narrative, which addresses the reader directly (for instance, *In case you're wondering*).

● Invite the children to find dialogue in the extract. Ask: *What has the author done instead of using direct speech?* (He has used the phrase *I told* to describe what happened instead.)

● Read aloud the part where Mom puts items on the table and Manny fetches the orange, noting that few words are spoken (only when Mom told Manny to point). Discuss the reasons why. (Because Manny was young, he would understand better by looking at real objects, also he copied Mom by getting a food item so didn't need words.)

● The text jumps from Manny getting the orange to Greg being sent to bed, leaving us to imagine what happened in between. Ask the children to work in pairs and suggest actions that might have occurred, or dialogue that might have been spoken, to fill in the gap.

> **Differentiation**
> **For older/more confident learners:** Encourage the children to rewrite the scene from Extract 2, including spoken dialogue.
> **For younger/less confident learners:** In pairs, invite the children to mime common gestures and facial expressions which their partner needs to supply suitable words to, such as a shrug means 'I don't know'.

Plot, character and setting

Making comparisons

Objective: To use syntax and context to build their store of vocabulary as they read for meaning.
What you need: Copies of *Diary of a Wimpy Kid*, a map of the world, dictionaries and photocopiable page 16.
Cross-curricular link: Geography.

What to do

● Inform the children that the story is set in America. Locate the United States on a map and show the distance from the UK.
● Explain that, although we speak the same language, there are some differences between British and American English. Ask the children to find a word on the first page that shows this difference (*Mom*) and ask what we use (mum).
● In the very first entry, highlight *grade levels* and *first grade*, which show a difference in the American school system. What do they mean? (first graders are aged 6–7.) Ask: *What is our version of elementary school?* (Primary school.)
● With the class, read the last entry for January. What American words can the children identify? (For example, *homeroom, first period, kindergartners* and *diaper*.) If they don't know the meanings, can they deduce from the context?
● Hand out photocopiable page 16 and invite the children to match British English words with the American English words from the novel.

Differentiation
For older/more confident learners: Challenge the children to make a list of at least ten other words that are different in the US to the UK.
For younger/less confident learners: Let the children concentrate on matching five of the words and allow them to ignore the last task.

A good friend?

Objective: To deduce characters' reasons for behaviour from their actions.
What you need: Copies of *Diary of a Wimpy Kid*, Extract 3 (from page 10), writing materials and photocopiable page 17.
Cross-curricular links: PSHE, drama.

What to do

● Read Extract 3, reminding the children that Greg and Rowley are best friends, and that Greg doesn't tell us about any other good friends in the whole of the school year. With the class, discuss Greg's behaviour as a best friend.
● Read aloud the continuation of the extract in the book up until Greg gets home and his Mom takes him for ice cream. What do the class think about Greg's behaviour towards Rowley in this section? Ask the children to work in pairs to devise questions to ask both Greg and Rowley in the hot-seat after this series of events.
● Choose a few of the children to take turns to sit in the hot-seat and answer the questions from the rest of the class. Follow up with a group discussion about why Greg behaves as he does, and what Rowley may now do as a result.
● Hand out photocopiable page 17, inviting the children to decide what each character thinks about Greg's actions. As a class, compare their answers.

Differentiation
For older/more confident learners: In pairs, ask the children to script and re-enact the conversation Mr Winsky has with Rowley.
For younger/less confident learners: Allow the children to concentrate on just three of the characters' opinions of Greg's actions, completing half of the photocopiable sheet.

Plot, character and setting

Who decides?

> **Objective:** To identify and summarise evidence from a text to support a hypothesis.
> **What you need:** Copies of *Diary of a Wimpy Kid*, photocopiable page 18, plain paper, glue sticks and scissors.
> **Cross-curricular link:** PSHE.

What to do

● Write the word 'Rules' on the board and ask the children what this means to them. How many different examples can they give of where there are rules? (For example, in school, in sport, at home, on the road, and so on.) Ask: *Who decides what the rules should be and what happens if they are broken?*

● Suggest that many of the incidents in the story are based around people making decisions and setting rules for how things should be.

● Hand out photocopiable page 18. Explain that each of the statement cards relates to an incident in the novel where decisions have been made by teachers, parents or the children themselves. The children's task is to sort the cards according to which group made the rules. In pairs, encourage the children to discuss their reasons.

● When the lists are completed, discuss the results as a class. What helped them to decide? How do they feel about each group's list? Is it fair or desirable for one set of people to decide on rules? How would they feel if parents chose the rules for games the children invented?

> **Differentiation**
> **For older/more confident learners:** Challenge the children to write a set of rules for their classroom, providing reasons for their rules.
> **For younger/less confident learners:** Limit the children to categorise half of the statements on the photocopiable sheet.

It always goes wrong

> **Objective:** To identify and make notes of the main points of sections of text.
> **What you need:** Copies of *Diary of a Wimpy Kid*, writing materials and large sheets of card.
> **Cross-curricular links:** PSHE, maths.

What to do

● Ask: *Can you recall a time in the novel when things go exactly the way Greg plans them?* Talk with the class about how things always seem to go wrong for him. Ask for a few examples.

● Arrange the children into groups, and ask them to scan the book, listing events where things go wrong for Greg. Do they understand how and why Greg is disappointed?

● Bring the class together to discuss why things don't go according to plan. Is it always Greg's fault, or is he just particularly unlucky? Might he have better results sometimes if he thought things through more thoroughly?

> **Differentiation**
> **For older/more confident learners:** Ask the children to select a few of the events in the story and think of alternative actions that might have resulted in more positive outcomes. Ask them to continue the opening 'If I was Greg, I would have…', writing their alternative suggestion.
> **For younger/less confident learners:** Encourage the children to scan the novel and list a few things that either go right or wrong for Rowley (such as, becoming the cartoonist for the school paper). Why is Rowley more successful?

How to be popular

● Can you help Greg to improve his image and become popular? Cut out the ideas below and organise them under the headings 'Things to do' and 'Things to avoid'.

Persuade your parents to buy you the latest style clothes.	Train hard so you become a really good runner.
Offer to help people when they are having problems.	Make friends with the most popular kids by always agreeing with them.
Try your hardest to please your teachers and stick to the rules.	Learn and tell lots of jokes to make people laugh.
Stay away from unpopular kids.	Make friends with girls and boys.
Only make friends with boys.	Only make friends with girls.
Show others that you don't care and dare to break the rules.	Laugh at other kids' jokes, even if they aren't funny.
Listen to the other kids when they moan, or tell boring stories.	Choose the best-looking kids to be your friends.
Compliment people when they look good.	Boast about your costly holidays and expensive toys and games.
Try to play fair and make sure everyone gets their turn.	Don't worry about how you look, just be friendly and helpful.

PHOTOCOPIABLE

SECTION
4

Making comparisons

● Match the American English words to the equivalent British English words.

American English	British English
Vacation	Front garden
Dumb	Nappy
Vice principal	Holiday
Front yard	Deputy head
Principal	School council
Store	Headteacher
Ma'am	Silly
Student government	Miss
Diaper	Shop

● What other American English words do you know? Write them below, with their British English equivalent.

American English	British English

Plot, character and setting

SECTION

4

A good friend?

● Consider Greg's behaviour in the incident with Rowley and the kindergarten children. In the table below, write what each of the characters might say if, or when, they discover the truth.

Character	Comment
Greg	
Rowley	
Mr Winsky (teacher)	
Mrs Irvine (angry parent)	
Mom	

● What would you say to Greg about his behaviour in this incident?

_____

_____

_____

_____

_____

_____

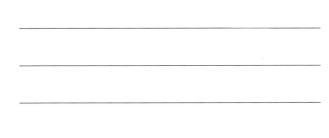

Illustration © 2007, Jeff Kinney.

Who decides?

● Create three columns with the headings 'Teachers', 'Children' and 'Parents'. Decide who makes each rule and place the cards below under the appropriate heading.

✂

Choosing Christmas presents.	Voting for the student government.	Making rules for household chores.
Deciding which children go into which groups.	Deciding what Halloween costumes are allowed.	Banning certain activities at home.
Choosing competition winners.	Setting punishments.	Deciding what is learned in school.
Deciding who goes trick-or-treating.	Making the rules for newly-invented games.	Choosing the winners of the school yearbook categories.
Deciding which video games are allowed.	Deciding that thank-you notes must be written.	Deciding on behaviour in the house.
Deciding what is allowed on posters.	Deciding personal music players are banned.	Making seating plans at the start of the year.
Deciding on what makes people popular.	Making the rules for 'The Cheese Touch'.	Deciding on auditioning for the school play.

● Compare your list with a partner and talk about how you made your decisions. Do you both agree?

■SCHOLASTIC
www.scholastic.co.uk

Talk about it

Trick or treat?

> **Objective:** To follow up others' points and show whether they agree or disagree in whole-class discussion.
> **What you need:** Copies of *Diary of a Wimpy Kid*.
> **Cross-curricular links:** PSHE, RE.

What to do
● With the class, read the first Monday's entry for October. Ask: *Why do you think Halloween is Greg's favourite holiday?* (It gives him an excuse for tricking people.)
● Talk about why Greg begins to have second thoughts about going into the haunted house when he arrives, and why Mom is in a hurry to get it over with.
● Organise a class discussion about the rights and wrongs of celebrating Halloween. Inform the children that Christians call it 'All Hallows' Eve', and it is the evening before All Saints' Day, but it has become a night for deliberately scaring people, especially children. Encourage the children to consider if it is just fun or might it really upset people, both children and adults. (For instance, Greg was scared of the chainsaw, and seemed relieved that Mom stepped in.) How might elderly people feel when trick-or-treaters call?
● Arrange them into pairs to discuss a scenario where trick-or-treating is banned. How would the children feel? Who might benefit from such a decision?

> **Differentiation**
> **For older/more confident learners:** Invite the children to present an oral case for or against trick-or-treating.
> **For younger/less confident learners:** Provide the children with a list of reasons for and against Halloween and, in pairs, ask them to decide which case each reason supports.

Let me explain…

> **Objective:** To sustain conversation, explain or give reasons for their views or language choices.
> **What you need:** Copies of *Diary of a Wimpy Kid*, two bats, a ball, toy bricks and writing materials.
> **Cross-curricular links:** PSHE, science.

What to do
● Read to the class the first Sunday's entry for October. Talk about the difficulty of trying to relate something visual using only words. Ask: *How easy was it for Greg to explain what was happening on the TV, and for Rowley to understand? What makes it difficult?* (For example, the speed of events, choosing the right words quickly, having no time for the listener to ask clarifying questions.)
● Take the class to the school hall and choose two of them to bat a ball between them. Explain that you will be asking for volunteers to commentate on the action, first discussing what language they might choose.
● Allow the group to watch the game for a short period before choosing commentators. Give each commentator five minute slots to explain the action.
● Afterwards, talk about the ease or difficulty of keeping up with the action.

> **Differentiation**
> **For older/more confident learners:** Invite pairs of children to sit opposite each other, with a barrier between them. One child should build a small model using toy bricks and then give oral instructions so the other can recreate the model. Compare results.
> **For younger/less confident learners:** Allow pairs of children to sit opposite each other with a barrier. One child should draw a house, giving instructions to their partner to recreate the drawing. Compare results.

Talk about it

Points of view

Objective: To create roles showing how behaviour can be interpreted from different viewpoints.
What you need: Copies of *Diary of a Wimpy Kid* and photocopiable page 22.
Cross-curricular links: PSHE, drama.

What to do

● With the class, read the first Tuesday's entry for November. (The Guided reading section provides help with specific vocabulary.)
● Greg is motivated to do something positive by the introduction of wrestling at school. His parents are pleased, but want to help him in different ways, neither of which appeal to Greg.
● Discuss with the children how each of the characters has a different perspective on the situation. Ask: *Is it possible to say if any one of the three is right?* Discuss their responses and reasons.

● Hand out photocopiable page 22 for the children to complete the speech bubbles in pairs. Once completed, they should join another pair and discuss their answers.
● Bring the class together and choose a few children to read out their speech captions. Encourage the rest of the class to work out whether the speaker is Mom, Dad or Greg, explaining their reasoning.

Differentiation
For older/more confident learners: Encourage the children to develop a monologue in role as one of the three characters, stating their point of view, with explanations about their opinions.
For younger/less confident learners: Allow the children to concentrate on writing two of the speech bubbles, providing sentence starters to help guide them.

Who would say that?

Objective: To use some drama strategies to explore stories or issues.
What you need: A copy of Extract 1 (from page 8) and photocopiable page 23.
Cross-curricular links: Drama, PSHE.

What to do

● Display and read Extract 1, about Greg trying out for the school play. In groups, ask the children to freeze-frame paragraphs 1, 3 and 6, selecting individuals to speak the thoughts of the characters they are portraying in each scenario.
● Talk about the language Greg might use in trying to persuade his parents to take his viewpoint. Might he choose different approaches depending on which parent he is speaking to? What might he say to each of them?

● Hand out photocopiable page 23, inviting the children to independently match the speech bubbles to the characters and examine the persuasive language.
● In pairs, the children should then compare their answers, and practise reading the comments in an appropriate tone of voice.
● As a class, share results and choose a few children to read out the various dialogues from the sheet.

Differentiation
For older/more confident learners: In groups of three, ask the children to act out the whole scene, using appropriate dialogue and intonation.
For younger/less confident learners: Allow the children to focus on matching half of the speech bubbles to the characters.

Talk about it

Rights and wrongs

Objective: To offer reasons and evidence for their views, considering alternative opinions.
What you need: A copy of Extract 2 (from page 9).
Cross-curricular links: PSHE, RE, drama.

What to do

● Display and read Extract 2. With the class, discuss Greg's behaviour towards his younger brother in this incident. Ask: *Is he wrong to pretend the thread is a spider, or is it just normal fun that brothers might engage in? Would Greg expect Manny to believe it is a spider?* Is Greg being cruel because he is bigger and older, or is he being a good brother by playing with Manny?
● Arrange the children into groups and provide them with time to talk about how Greg, Manny and Mom might feel about the situation. Would Greg think Manny was a sneak, and unfair? Would Manny feel that Greg was being a bully? Would Mom be worried and upset that Greg appeared to be terrorising his brother?
● Draw the discussion together as a class, eliciting the children's responses to the group discussion. Ask: *Was Greg right or wrong to do what he did? What reasons do you have for your opinion?*

Differentiation
For older/more confident learners: Invite the children to take the hot-seat in role as Greg and to answer questions from the group, to ascertain his thoughts on the incident, including his punishment. (How would Greg feel if Rodrick had done it to him?)
For younger/less confident learners: Ask the children to discuss suitable ways for siblings to play together.

Author interview

Objective: To sustain conversation, explain or give reasons for their views or choices.
What you need: A copy of Extract 3 (from page 10), internet access and photocopiable page 24.
Cross-curricular links: PSHE, ICT.

What to do

● Display and read Extract 3. Point out that this is just one example of Greg's questionable behaviour, and ask the class for others. What words would they use to describe Greg? (Perhaps selfish, uncaring, unfeeling, thoughtless.)
● Jeff Kinney says on his website that Greg is not a good role model. Discuss why he would choose to write about him. Ask: *Would Greg be classed as the hero of the story? How would parents feel about their children reading about a character such as Greg? Could Greg be there to show us how not to behave?* (After all, he rarely seems to be successful, and doesn't seem to have any real friends.)
● Show the children the interview with the author on his website: (www.wimpykid.com) and the links to other interviews he has given (in the video and audio section).
● Hand out photocopiable page 24 and encourage the children to complete it by composing questions to ask the author.

Differentiation
For older/more confident learners: Allow the children to research Jeff Kinney from other internet sources, including other interviews he has given. In small groups they should collate their information and present it to the class.
For younger/less confident learners: Let the children concentrate on writing three questions under the headings provided on the photocopiable sheet.

Points of view

● Mom, Dad and Greg have different ideas about how Greg should get fit. Talk about their ideas with a partner, using the word bank to help you. Then write in the speech bubbles what Mom, Dad and Greg might say to present their point of view on the subject.

Dad says:

Mum says:

Greg says

Word bank

gain weight	increase muscle	get fitter
exercise equipment	weight-gain powder	muscle magazines
enthusiastic	work out regularly	exercise regime
sit-ups	jumping jacks	high-tech machines
bench press	Christmas	Fregley

● Now discuss your answers with another pair.

READ & RESPOND: Activities based on *Diary of a Wimpy Kid*

Who would say that?

● Read the speech bubbles, cut them out and match them to the correct characters (listed below). Then discuss the most powerful and persuasive words. Practise reading each one aloud.

Greg	Mom	Dad

I think it would be a great idea to try out for the school play. Think how popular it would make you!

Do I really have to do this? It would be so embarrassing. My friends would laugh at me.

This wouldn't keep him fit and healthy. It would get completely in the way of the weightlifting schedule.

But you have such a wonderful singing voice! It would make me so proud to see you in the play.

I always wanted to see my son do well at sports. It's character building.

But that flyer wasn't meant for kids in my class. It was a mistake that I brought it home.

Please, I beg you, don't make me do this. I'd be so miserable and worried that I wouldn't get any sleep.

You need new experiences to make you well-rounded. How will you ever know what you're good at if you don't try?

Author interview

● Imagine you are going to interview the author Jeff Kinney about *Diary of a Wimpy Kid*. Under each of the headings below, write the questions you would like to ask him.

The character of Greg	Greg's actions
How Greg behaves towards his friends	How Greg's parents deal with his behaviour
Adults' views about the book	The character of Rowley
Any other question	Any other question

● Now compare your questions with a partner. What do you think Jeff Kinney's answers might be?

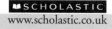

Get writing

Halloween plans

Objective: To use layout, format, graphics and illustrations for different purposes.
What you need: Copies of *Diary of a Wimpy Kid*, writing materials, individual whiteboards and paper.
Cross-curricular link: ICT.

What to do

● Examine with the class the haunted house plans (detailed in the first Saturday's entry for October). Ask the children what they notice about how the plan is organised (such as arrows guide the way through, illustrations are briefly annotated, the exit is marked, writing is in clear block capitals).

● Discuss the ideas Greg and Rowley have for their haunted house and where they might have come from (prior knowledge of Halloween, their reading/viewing, their imagination). Can the children suggest any other ideas that could have been included?

● Invite the children to design their own haunted house in a similar diagrammatic form. Encourage them to devise their own ideas and allow time for partners to discuss what to include and for initial plans to be created, before making their final plan.

Differentiation
For older/more confident learners: Ask the children to explain the difficulties of actually making some of the scenes in their own or Greg's plan.
For younger/less confident learners: Let the children concentrate on two items for their haunted house and draw detailed diagrams, perhaps with further explanatory annotations.

Build your body!

Objective: To summarise and shape material and ideas from different sources to write convincing and informative non-narrative texts.
What you need: Copies of *Diary of a Wimpy Kid*, photocopiable page 28, paper and writing materials.
Cross-curricular links: PE, ICT.

What to do

● Remind the children about how Greg is keen to gain strength and skill in order to do well in the school wrestling unit (see November entries). Ask: *What is involved in Greg's plan to achieve his goal?* Make a list on the board of the children's suggestions.

● Talk about how effective Greg's ideas might have been if he had done them well, and ask for any other suggestions the children might be able to offer.

● Explain that they are going to make a leaflet on a folded sheet of A4, which will outline ideas for what Greg and his classmates could do to build their bodies in preparation for the wrestling unit.

● Tell the children that they can use ideas from the story or their own ideas.

● Hand out photocopiable page 28 on which the children should record their research. They should then use their notes to help create their leaflets.

Differentiation
For older/more confident learners: Encourage the children to use a computer to make their leaflets, including images to enhance the text.
For younger/less confident learners: Allow the children to focus on researching three areas from the sheet and work in pairs to write their leaflets.

Get writing

Thank you

Objective: To compose sentences using adjectives, verbs and nouns for precision, clarity and impact.
What you need: Copies of *Diary of a Wimpy Kid*, writing materials, envelopes and thesauruses.
Cross-curricular link: PSHE.

What to do

● Read the first Thursday entry for January, where Greg is writing his thank-you letters. Discuss Greg's method for doing this, and why it didn't work. Talk about the need to personalise letters, such as mentioning the gift, saying how it will be appreciated or used and referring to something the writer shares with the giver.

● Ask the children to suggest some gifts that they might receive at Christmas – both those they want and those they don't. List the gifts on the board in two columns labelled 'Want' and 'Don't want'. Briefly discuss how the recipient might respond in a thank-you letter to the giver.

● Invite the children to choose a gift from each column, and to write a thank-you letter for each, to a fictional giver. Encourage careful use of vocabulary, to suit the giver (one giver should be a child and one an adult) and the present. The letters should be written on paper and put into envelopes.

● When all letters are complete, deliver them randomly to the class, who should read them out. Then as a class discuss how the letters appear to the recipients.

Differentiation
For older/more confident learners: Encourage the children to use similes and adverbs to improve the descriptive qualities of the letters.
For younger/less confident learners: Provide the children with a list of useful adjectives and thesauruses.

Rowley's journal

Objective: To show imagination through the language used to create emphasis, humour, atmosphere or suspense.
What you need: Copies of *Diary of a Wimpy Kid*, photocopiable page 29 and writing materials.
Cross-curricular links: PSHE, drama.

What to do

● Remind the children that, because the novel is a journal written in the first person, we learn about everything from the writer's (Greg's) point of view. However, other people are always involved in what he records and they may see events differently.

● As an example, read the very first Thursday's entry and ask for suggestions about how Rodrick and Dad would relate the incident. (Probably Rodrick would think it was funny, while Dad would be angry, annoyed and unsure who to believe.)

● Talk about the way that Greg treats his friend Rowley, and write on the board any words or phrases the children suggest for his behaviour (such as 'selfish', 'mean', 'thoughtless', 'cruel', 'unfair').

● Read the first entry for January and ask for suggestions for what Rowley might say about the 'Big Wheel' incident.

● Hand out photocopiable page 29 and explain that they need to choose one incident, consider Rowley's version of events and write in role as Rowley.

Differentiation
For older/more confident learners: Ask the children to imagine a scenario where Greg finds Rowley's written version of events, and then to write Greg's reaction to it.
For younger/less confident learners: Encourage the children to write a short paragraph and include simple cartoons to enhance writing.

Get writing

Cartoon kid

Objective: To choose and combine words, images and other features for particular effects.
What you need: Copies of *Diary of a Wimpy Kid* and writing materials.
Cross-curricular link: Art.

What to do

● Remind the class of the book's subtitle, *A novel in cartoons*. Talk about how the simple illustrations add to both our understanding and enjoyment of the story.

● Explain to the children that the cartoons are very simple, focusing on the characters, whose faces show emotions by the use of simple lines. There are few background features, they only exist when they are needed for the context to be clear (such as the classroom, home or street). Note also the use of speech bubbles, with words written in the customary block capitals.

● Ask the children to think of an incident that has happened to them at school that others would find interesting or amusing. They should briefly tell a partner their story before portraying it in a cartoon strip.

● Invite them to fold a piece of paper into eight sections and create a cartoon in eight parts.

● To support the children, on the board write these key points for them to remember: simple drawings, facial expressions, limited backgrounds, speech bubbles and capital letters.

Differentiation
For older/more confident learners: Using the second Thursday entry for February as reference, challenge the children to create their own fictional cartoon strip, suitable for a school magazine.
For younger/less confident learners: Allow the children to create a cartoon with only four to six sections.

Class yearbook

Objective: To use settings and characterisation to engage readers' interest.
What you need: Copies of *Diary of a Wimpy Kid* and photocopiable page 30.
Cross-curricular links: Drama, art.

What to do

● Show the class the pictures from the school yearbook, which can be found in the first Monday's entry for April and at the end of the novel. Do they know what a yearbook is? (A book that records highlights of the past school year, and celebrates individuals' widely varied achievements and potential.) Encourage suggestions for the titles and awards that people might be given (such as most likely to succeed, best athlete and top musician).

● On the board, list the names of the six main characters (Greg, Rowley, Rodrick, Fregley, Greg's Mom and Dad). Ask the children what

the key characteristics are for each one and briefly list their responses. What might the highlights of the year have been for each character, their best moments or achievements?

● Hand out photocopiable page 30 and explain that they are going to create a yearbook entry for each character.

● In pairs, the children should talk about what title each character might be awarded, making notes before completing the sheet. Simple illustrations should also be included.

Differentiation
For older/more confident learners: Invite the children to extend the characters' entries to half a page each and to add additional entries for minor characters (such as Manny) on a separate sheet.
For younger/less confident learners: Limit the children to create yearbook entries for three of the characters.

Build your body!

● Research how to build your body and improve fitness levels. Use the table below to make notes and use this information to create a leaflet that Greg might have found useful when training for the school wrestling unit.

Exercises:	Equipment:
Diet:	Training programmes:
Keeping a record:	Working with a partner:

Here is a list of possible search words to use during your research:

Word bank:	getting fit	building muscles
fitness regimes	body-building	weight training
diet for health	gym workouts	keep-fit exercises

Rowley's journal

- Choose one of these four incidents from the story:
  - Trick-or-treating
  - Weight training
  - Teasing the kindergartners
  - Building the snowman

- Imagine how Rowley would interpret the incident. Make brief notes from both Greg's and Rowley's points of view. Use your notes to write Rowley's own journal entry for your chosen incident.

Greg	Rowley

Rowley's journal entry:

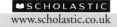

Class yearbook

- Imagine you are creating a class yearbook. Write the end of year entry for each of these characters from *Diary of a Wimpy Kid.* Include the award you would give each one and draw a picture of them.

Rowley
Entry:

Award:

Greg's Dad
Entry:

Award:

Fregley
Entry:

Award:

Greg
Entry:

Award:

Greg's Mom
Entry:

Award:

Rodrick
Entry:

Award:

Assessment

Assessment advice

As the children read *Diary of a Wimpy Kid*, use the questions and prompts from Section 2 to assess their understanding of the text. The children should keep notes on each character as they read, to describe differences in their personalities and their attitudes towards Greg, and Greg's attitudes towards each of them. Do the children understand why Greg is so honest in what he writes, when he has told us that he intends to use his journal to tell the general public about himself when he is 'rich and famous'? (He doesn't realise that what he does and how he treats people might be viewed as unacceptable.) Ask the children if they think there is anything that Greg might give a different version of when he looks back as an older person, and how he might change the details of what he wrote. (As an adult he may realise that his actions and attitudes were questionable.)

Invite the class to consider why this form of writing appeals to readers (it speaks directly to us, we feel we are being let in on something private and we also enjoy the humour). Did the children experience any difficulties in their understanding of the text? (For example, the American and specialised vocabulary or the unfamiliar setting.) How did they tackle this? Would they recommend the book to others? If so, to whom and why, or why not?

School report card

> **Assessment focus:** To interrogate texts to deepen and clarify understanding and response.
> **What you need:** Copies of *Diary of a Wimpy Kid*, photocopiable page 32 and writing materials.

What to do

● After finishing the book, ask for the children's opinions about Greg, giving their reasons. When do they have positive feelings towards him or feel sympathy for his situation, and why? Have they had experiences similar to Greg which make them empathise with him?

● Ask: *Which parts of the story gave negative feelings about Greg and why? Can you suggest any ways in which Greg could adapt his attitude and behaviour so that he gets into less trouble and enjoys more success?*

● Discuss the way other characters in the story react to Greg's actions. Do the children think their own friends, families and teachers would behave in the ways described? Are the events related in the story believable? If so, what gives them their authenticity and, if not, what makes particular events less plausible?

● Remind the children that Greg's journal covers a school year. Hand out photocopiable page 32 and ask them to imagine they are Greg's form teacher, and to complete an end of year school report for him. Talk about the need to be both positive and honest when examining Greg.

● When assessing the children's work, look for evidence that they can identify and accurately portray Greg's character, supported by examples from the text. For example, Greg put in great effort to do well in the wrestling unit but had a poor attitude when looking after kindergarteners during Safety Patrol.

School report card

Imagine you are Greg's teacher. Consider the events of the school year and write Greg's end of year report for his parents.

KT-9

REPORT CARD

Pupil's name: Greg Heffley

Strengths:	Areas for development:
Attitude to school and work:	**Effort:**
Behaviour:	**Summary of the year:**

Signed: _____